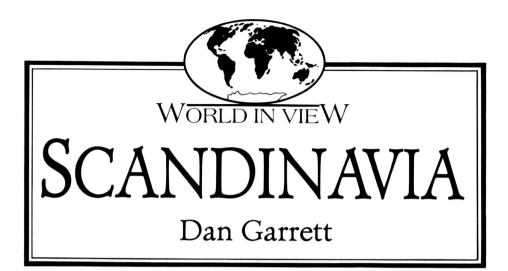

WORLD IN VIEW

SCANDINAVIA

Dan Garrett

STECK-VAUGHN
L I B R A R Y

Austin, Texas

Library of Congress Cataloging-in-Publication Data

Garrett, Dan, 1941-
   Scandinavia / Dan Garrett.
      p.   cm.—(World in view)
   Includes index.
   Summary: Surveys the history, climate, geography, culture, religion, and economics of the people of Denmark, Norway, Sweden, Finland, and Iceland.
   ISBN 0-8114-2444-8
   1. Scandinavia—Juvenile literature. [1. Scandinavia.]
   I. Title. II. Series.
DL5.G36   1991
948—dc20   91-6422
                                       CIP AC

Cover: *Fedafjord, Norway*
Title page: *Ålesund, Norway*

Designed by Julian Holland Publishing Ltd
Picture research by Jennifer Johnson

Typeset by Multifacit Graphics, Keyport, NJ
Printed and bound in the United States
by Lake Book, Melrose Park, IL
1 2 3 4 5 6 7 8 9 0 LB 95 94 93 92 91

Photographic credits
Cover: Tony Stone (Robert Everts), title page: B. Gerard/Hutchison Library, 5, 7, 9 G. Sherlock, 10 Dan Garrett, 12 J. Allan Cash, 15 Dan Garrett, 16 G. Sherlock, 17 Dan Garrett, 19 G. Sherlock, 20 Joulumaa/Santa Claus Land, 23 G. Sherlock, 24, 25 Dan Garrett, 27 Malvik, 32 Dan Garrett, 33, 35, 37, 39 G. Sherlock, 40 Dan Garrett, 42, 45, 47, 48, 49, 50 G. Sherlock, 53 Bernard Régent/Hutchison Library, 55 J. Allan Cash, 56, 57, 61 G. Sherlock, 63 Markku Juntunen/Finnish Tourist Board, 65 Hutchison Library, 67, 68, 70 Dan Garrett, 72 G. Sherlock, 76 Bridgeman Art Library, 77 G. Sherlock, 81 Dan Garrett, 82, 85 G. Sherlock, 87 Hutchison Library, 89 Swedish National Tourist Office, 93 A. Heinila/Finnish Tourist Board.

Acknowledgments
I would like to thank my many friends of the Nordic Conference of the European Broadcasting Union, and in particular Seppo Korhonen of Finnish Educational Radio, Margareta Hallberg and Brenda Bennett of Swedish Educational Broadcasting, and Rolv Skarstein and Hege Jensen of Norwegian Educational Broadcasting. Warrill Grindrod and Bob Dixon have given invaluable help with the manuscript.

Contents

Pronunciation Guide

Å — "aw" as in "awe"
Ä, ä — "e" as in "get"
fj — "fe" as in "fee"
j — "y" as in "yours"
ø, ö — "er" as in "earth"

SCANDINAVIA

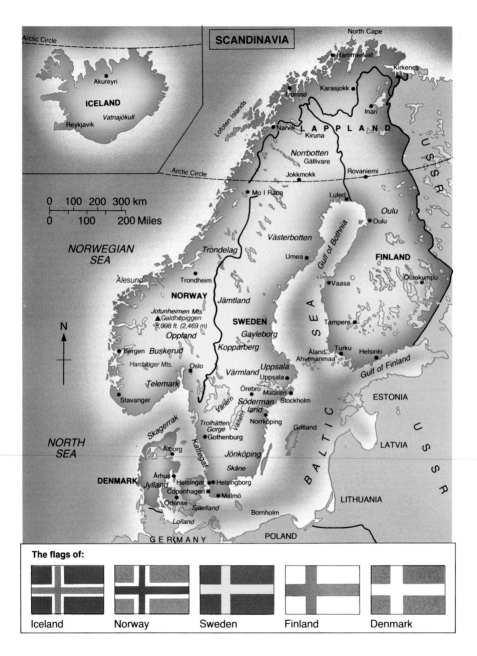

The flags of:

| Iceland | Norway | Sweden | Finland | Denmark |

1 What Is Scandinavia?

The word Scandinavia is used in a very general way. Often it is in connection with house interiors, as in Scandinavian furniture, or Scandinavian design. Used in this way, it brings to mind warm rooms with sleek pine furniture looking out onto snowy landscapes dotted with fir trees.

Geographers define the Scandinavian Peninsula as the arm of land pointing south from the northwestern Soviet Union toward Britain and Germany. Norway and Sweden are the main countries on the peninsula. Many people use the term Scandinavia more generally, to describe the five countries that have been very closely

The deep inlets or fjords along the coast of Norway were gouged out by glaciers during the Ice Age. Most fjords are surrounded by steep snowcapped mountains, and the easiest way to travel from fjord to fjord is by sea.

Fact Box

Denmark

Area:	16,638 square miles (43,093 sq. kilometers)
Population:	5,129,254
Currency:	the Danish *krone*, which is divided into 100 *øre*

Finland

Area:	140,781 square miles (364,623 sq. kilometers)
Population:	4,938,602
Official language:	Finnish and Swedish
Currency:	the *mark*, divided into 100 *pennis*

Iceland

Area:	39,698 square miles (102,819 sq. kilometers)
Population:	247,357
Currency:	the *króna* (plural *Krónur*), divided into 1,000 *eyrir* (plural *aurar*)

Norway

Area:	125,049 square miles (323,877 sq. kilometers)
Population:	4,198,300
Official language:	Bokmål (or Riksmål) and Nynorsk (or Landsmål)
Currency:	the Norwegian *krone* (plural *kroner*), divided into 100 *øre*

Sweden

Area:	158,659 square miles (410,928 sq. kilometers)
Population:	8,414,083
Currency:	the Swedish *krona*, divided into 100 *øre*

Since early times Scandinavians have had to rely on ships to cross the surrounding seas and make contact with the rest of the world. Most of their biggest cities are also important ports.

connected for over 1,000 years: Denmark, Iceland, Finland, Norway, and Sweden. This is the way the word is used in this book. The people who live in these countries often call them the Nordic Countries, the Countries of the North.

The Arctic Circle is an imaginary line circling the Earth at just under 67° of latitude north of the equator. It passes through Norway, Sweden, and Finland, and just grazes the northern capes of Iceland. Its position is often marked by roadside signs or sculptures.

Lands surrounded by seas

Scandinavia is surprisingly large. Northward from the Danish border with Germany to Norway's North Cape is a distance of 1,300 miles

Midwinter Darkness and Midnight Sun

The amount of daylight a place gets depends on the way the Earth's axis is tilted relative to the sun. During autumn in the northern hemisphere, the North Pole gradually tilts farther and farther away from the sun, so the days get shorter and shorter.

In the southern hemisphere, the same thing happens, except six months later. In April and May, during the southern autumn, the South Pole tilts farther and farther away from the sun, giving shorter days in Antarctica.

In late December, there is one day when the sun does not rise at all at places on the Arctic Circle. A dawnlike glow brightens in the south, but not even the rim of the sun manages to break the midwinter skyline. After a while, the glow fades, and night returns for another 24 hours. North of the Arctic Circle, the darkness is continuous for weeks or even months, depending on the closeness of the area to the North Pole.

In summer, it is just the reverse. From March, the days lengthen rapidly, until, on Midsummer's Day in June, the sun does not set at all at the Arctic Circle. Farther north, unbroken daylight lasts for days, weeks, and even months. The sun simply circles the sky, reaching its highest point in the south at midday. At midnight, it is still warming the land from a low point on the northern horizon.

The northern summer may only last for a brief while, but the long days are important to Scandinavia. Plants, animals, and people all seem to respond in a great burst of energy and activity.

During the summer, the sun never sets north of the Arctic Circle, and places such as Alvundfoss are bathed in light even at midnight.

(2,300 kilometers). Measured south from the Danish border, that same distance would stretch to the coast of North Africa. Another surprise is that there are only two connections with the rest of Europe of any use to someone traveling by land. These are between Germany and Denmark, and between Leningrad in the Soviet Union and Helsinki in Finland.

The sea almost surrounds the Scandinavian countries. To the north is the Barents Sea, which is part of the Arctic Ocean. To the west are the Norwegian and North seas. To the south and east is the landlocked Baltic and its eastward extension, the Gulf of Finland. The Gulf of Bothnia is the northern arm of the Baltic between Finland and Sweden. These sea barriers have made ships vital to the Scandinavians, and most of their biggest cities are important ports. From Denmark it is 300 miles (500 kilometers) across the North Sea to Britain. Iceland is an isolated island in the Atlantic Ocean, 600 miles (1,000 kilometers) west of Norway, but the Danish Faeroe Islands are like a halfway stepping-stone. They are a welcome sight to sailors braving the northern

The Lofoten Islands are off the coast of northwestern Norway. These isolated, mist-shrouded islands were formed from mountain ranges that were drowned by the rise of the sea when the Ice Age ended.

seas in winter. When those sailors reach Iceland, they are halfway to Greenland, and not much less than halfway to North America.

Mountains, fjords, islands, and lakes

A range of mountains runs down the western side of the Scandinavian Peninsula like a spine. Where these mountains drop into the Norwegian Sea, steep-sided, sea-filled valleys, or fjords, cut deep into them. The mountains are of hard rocks that make a jagged, imposing landscape. The Lofoten Islands off northern Norway are a drowned westerly ridge of the same range and rise out of the sea mist like strange monsters.

The mountains of Scandinavia are highest in southern Norway, where they are snow-covered all year round. Beneath the mountain peaks are glaciers, such as the Hardangerjøkul, which are leftovers from the last Ice Age. (*Jøkul* is Norwegian for glacier.) Eastward, the mountain range slopes into Sweden. Regularly spaced rivers run southeast, taking rainwater and melted snow into the Baltic. Southern Sweden and Finland are comparatively flat, although, particularly in Finland, there are chains of gravel hills left over from the Ice Age. Denmark is the flattest Scandinavian country.

Central Sweden is broken up by large freshwater lakes, some more than 50 miles (80 kilometers) long, such as Vänern and Mälaren. In total, Sweden has around 100,000 lakes, making up six percent of the country's area. Finland has even more, a total of 188,000 lakes, making up ten percent of its area.

Also typical of Scandinavia are the many islands. Two of Denmark's main provinces, Sjaelland and Fyn, are islands. On a map they look like stepping-stones between Jylland (the part of Denmark jutting out from Germany) and Sweden. Most of Scandinavia's long coastlines have chains of islands, or archipelagos. Stretching across the Gulf of Bothnia between Sweden and Finland are the Finnish islands of Ahvenanmaa, Åland in Swedish.

Island of ice and fire

Iceland more than lives up to its name. Much of the center is covered by glaciers and snowfields. The island's largest glacier is Vatnajökull. In summer, the snows melt to reveal a bleak, gray, moonlike landscape. This is the result of lava flows; Iceland lies in one of the world's active volcanic regions. In 1963 lava rose up out of the sea to form the new island of Surtsey, Black Island. Ten years later, the 500 inhabitants of the offshore Westman Islands had to be moved when a huge crack blew open. However, Icelanders get

The volcanic terrain of Iceland offers some fascinating attractions to tourists. There are hot springs and geysers that throw water and steam high above the nearly treeless landscape. The Strokkur Geyser is one of the most spectacular.

natural compensation for the problems caused by the volcanoes. Hot springs called geysers spurt into the air, making pools warm enough to swim in even in the middle of winter, and also providing hot water for many homes.

Population spread

The Scandinavian climate makes life in the north very hard. For this reason, most towns and cities are in southern Scandinavia. Many of the main towns, Helsinki and Turku in Finland, Stockholm in Sweden, and Oslo and Bergen in Norway, are all about 60° north. The small populations and the need to keep as much land as possible for farming mean that Scandinavian cities are

12

compact. There are few suburban sprawls, except for Ørestad, based on Copenhagen in Denmark, and Malmö in Sweden. Closely linked towns and cities sprawl along both sides of Øresund, the narrow stretch of water separating the two countries.

Scandinavia has a large land area for its population, and outside the cities it is noticeable how thinly towns and villages are scattered. Iceland, Norway, and Finland are the three most sparsely populated countries in Europe. There is a great sense of space, and hikers can go for days in a wilderness of birch trees and lakes without seeing a single person.

Population

Denmark 304 persons per square mile
(119 per square kilometer)
Finland 37 persons per square mile
(15 per square kilometer)
Iceland 6 persons per square mile
(2.4 per square kilometer)
Norway 33 persons per square mile
(13 per square kilometer)
Sweden 49 persons per square mile
(19 per square kilometer)

For comparison, the United States has 64 persons per square mile (25 per square kilometer), Britain has 643 persons per square mile (351 per square kilometer), and Australia has an average of 5 persons per square mile (2 per square kilometer).

2

Snowdrifts, Fir Trees, and the Saami

It is surprising that people find it possible to live as far north as they do in Scandinavia. Much of the land lies between latitudes 60° and 70° north, and if the space between these latitudes is traced around the world, it includes vast, almost uninhabited regions in the Soviet Union, Canada, and Alaska. However, Scandinavia is warmer in winter than these places.

Climate

There are two main reasons for Scandinavia's milder winters. The first reason is the closeness of the sea, which cools much more slowly in winter than the land and keeps the region warmer. In addition, the sea current called the North Atlantic Drift, moving up across the Atlantic Ocean from the Caribbean, warms Norway's west coast as it does the west coast of Britain. The second reason

Temperature
Stockholm's average temperature of 65°F (18°C) is the same as London's, which is considerably farther south. The Swedish town of Kiruna, north of the Arctic Circle, has 2,000 hours of sunshine per year. This is 500 less than New York, but 500 more than London.
   Reykjavik, the capital of Iceland, is also affected by the warm North Atlantic Drift. In January, it is warmer on average, at 30.2°F (-1°C), than New York or Vienna.

Bergen on the west coast of Norway has been a bustling port for centuries. Among Norwegians, however, one of its main claims to fame is its heavy rainfall.

for the milder winters is that most winds come from the west and southwest. They are comparatively mild because of their journey over the Atlantic.

The drawback is that these winds have picked up large amounts of moisture from the sea. In winter, this falls as very deep snow on the high mountains just inland from Norway's coast. The then-drier winds sweep on into Sweden, where snowfalls are less than in Norway, though still a lot compared with many countries! In summer, the same southwesterly winds tend to make Norway and Denmark cloudier and rainier than the rest of Scandinavia. Bergen, Norway's most westerly port, has an annual rainfall of 78.3 inches (1,958 millimeters). Norwegians say, "It's always

15

Copenhagen, the capital of Denmark, along with all the other Scandinavian capitals, has a cold winter with snow for several months. During the coldest months even the sea freezes.

raining in Bergen." Eastern Scandinavia's climate is more influenced by the very cold winters and hot summers of central Europe. Sweden and Finland enjoy sunny and often quite dry and hot summers.

In Iceland and the far north of Norway and Finland, the climate is influenced by the polar ice and winds. In winter, drifting ice forms around the coast of Iceland and northern Norway, while the gulfs of Bothnia and Finland often freeze over completely. Icebreakers are needed to make channels for other ships to reach ports and harbors like Helsinki.

Trees south to north

Trees give one of the clearest signs of how Scandinavia's climate varies. In the south, there is a mix of trees, both broad-leaved and coniferous. Farther north, in central Sweden, Norway, and Finland, fir trees and other conifers blanket the land in dark forests. Nearer the Arctic Circle, the fir trees begin to give way to birch, the hardiest of all trees. North of the Arctic Circle, even the birch has a hard time. With every mile farther north, the trees become more and more stunted, because there is so little growing time each year. Even fully grown birch trees are more like bushes. In Iceland, the climate is so harsh that there are very few trees at all. The island, like the very north of Norway, looks bleak and barren.

In central Sweden there is a good variety of both deciduous and coniferous trees. However, toward the north, the number and variety of trees decrease until there are only the stunted bushes and mosses of the tundra.

The Northern Lights
Scandinavia in winter can be a good place to see the spectacular light patterns that occur high in the Earth's atmosphere at certain times. The Aurora Borealis, or Northern Lights, are caused by energy-charged particles from the sun being trapped in the Earth's magnetic field. The fast-moving particles cause atoms in the atmosphere to give off light. The lights appear as a strange flickering glow spreading across the sky. They change colors, but are usually in shades of green or red.

Wildlife

About 10,000 years ago Scandinavia was buried under ice. Century by century the weather became slightly warmer, the glaciers retreated into the higher mountains, and the Ice Age came to an end. Trees and plants returned, and animals began to migrate northward from warmer countries. Scandinavia, like Russia, became populated with elk, reindeer, bears, wolves, and other animals adapted to cold climates.

Wolves and a few hundred bears still roam some of the remoter parts of Scandinavia. Reindeer and elk run wild over most of Norway, Sweden, and Finland, and warning signs are common along roads. Even as far south as Oslo, a cross-country skier can meet an elk.

Many of the common European birds, such as sparrows, starlings, blackbirds, titmice, and thrushes, are also found in Scandinavia. Parts of Denmark are far enough south to attract storks, and in some villages near the German border,

A variety of wildlife lives in the vast forests of Scandinavia and can be a problem to motorists. The largest of these animals is the elk, which can be over six feet (two meters) high at the shoulder. Road signs warn motorists about the possibility of meeting one of these huge creatures crossing the road.

farmers still put up cartwheels on poles to encourage the birds to nest. In the more northern and mountainous parts of Scandinavia there are gamebirds capable of living in snowbound forests, such as grouse and ptarmigan, and birds of prey like eagles. In central Scandinavia, lakes attract a great variety of wildfowl and the coastlines are havens for seabirds.

Seals are common on Norway's Atlantic coast, although recently many have died, partly because of pollution. Whaling used to be an important Norwegian industry, but so few whales are left that Norway, like almost all nations, has stopped hunting them. Sadly, Iceland continues, giving as a reason that the hunting is for "scientific reasons," but in fact exporting the meat to Japan.

The Saami

As the Ice Age ended, hunters followed the animals into Scandinavia, and began to live there. One group that moved into Finland learned how to herd reindeer. They were the Saami or, as others used to call them, the Lapps. Almost all of their livelihood came from the reindeer. They used its meat for food and its hide for clothing, footwear, and for covering tents, which were made much like the teepees of native North Americans.

Over centuries, the Finns and Norwegians pushed the Saami farther and farther to the north, where those who are left still live. Their land, Lappland, has no boundaries of its own, but covers parts of Norway, Sweden, and Finland. Most of the Saami now live in houses and only

The Saami, who live in Lappland, the traditional home of Santa Claus, use reindeer for food, clothing, and to carry their belongings. The Saami still wear their colorful costumes on occasion and every tribe has its own particular style of cap.

about 800 families still herd reindeer, making a living by selling the meat. Some of these families still live a nomadic life for part of the year, following the herds and living in tents.

All reindeer in Lappland belong to one Saami tribe or another, and the more reindeer a family owns, the wealthier it is. Each year, families round up their herds to check and count them. This is a way of seeing how rich they are. At this annual roundup, Saami on skis or snowmobiles, helped by reindeer dogs, drive the deer into wire enclosures. The old reindeer are slaughtered for meat, and calves are marked to show their owners. The roundup is an important social occasion and the Saami dress up in their brightly colored traditional costumes. Once, these used to be worn all year round, but today the traditional clothes are only brought out for special occasions such as the roundup and weddings.

The Saami suffered a big setback in 1986. Radioactive fallout from the fire at the Chernobyl nuclear power station in the Soviet Union blew over Lappland. The fallout contaminated the mossy plants called lichens that are eaten by the reindeer. As a result, the reindeer meat became radioactive. The Saami were not allowed to sell this meat, because it was too dangerous to eat, and consequently they lost a great deal of money.

3

The Vikings and Their Ancestors

The early peoples of the North were known as Norsemen. Norse or Nordic are old words for the North and are still used today to describe Scandinavian languages. The word "Viking" possibly comes from the Norse word *vik*, which means a bay or creek, and some historians think this is how the Vikings got their name. They are the "men from the creeks." Other historians say the evidence for this theory is not very strong. The word Viking now conjures up a picture of helmeted warriors in beautiful but sinister longboats, sailing up rivers to plunder and burn far inland. In deciding whether this is a true picture of early Scandinavians, it is important to remember that this description comes, not from the Vikings themselves, but from people who suffered from their raids.

Early Scandinavians

Our knowledge of the earliest Scandinavians comes from archaeological remains. The peat bogs in Denmark and central Sweden have preserved ancient leather and woolen items, such as shoes and clothing. The peat has even preserved the body of a man, thrown in the bog over 2,000 years ago. The expression on his face is still clear, and the rope around his neck is a gruesome clue to the way he died.

Excavations of early graves have revealed bowls and jugs, brooches, and bronze figures of

This beautiful Viking longship is now exhibited in a museum in Oslo, Norway. Chieftains were buried in their ships, many of which have been preserved in the ground. Boats similar to this one were used by the intrepid Vikings to explore across the Atlantic Ocean and as far south as Africa and the Mediterranean.

gods. Some luxury goods were imported from Rome and a Roman writer has described Scandinavian ships with a prow at both ends. The Scandinavian ships probably unloaded furs, reindeer skins, cattle, and sealskin ropes at a north German port, and then loaded up with Roman wine and cases of glass and bronzeware, all destined for some wealthy chieftain across the Baltic in what is now Sweden.

Life in early Scandinavia

The archaeological evidence gives a picture of southern Scandinavians in the period between about A.D. 400 and 800. Inland, they were farmers, growing rye, barley, and especially root crops like turnips and rutabagas, as well as keeping cattle

The Magical Runes

Scandinavian gravestones and weapons dating from 400 onward often have strange writing on them. The letters used in this writing, called runes, are made with mainly straight lines, which are easy to cut into wood or stone. When people who used the Roman alphabet saw runic writing, many of them thought it must be magical. In fact, once somebody has leaned the runic alphabet, inscriptions can be read quite easily.

There are runestones all over southern Scandinavia. Often they were put up as a memorial. Runic writing was used in remote parts of Scandinavia until the nineteenth century.

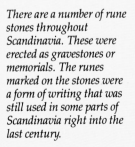

There are a number of rune stones throughout Scandinavia. These were erected as gravestones or memorials. The runes marked on the stones were a form of writing that was still used in some parts of Scandinavia right into the last century.

Fishing has been an important part of Scandinavian life for hundreds of years, and traditional methods are still used in many areas. On Ballstad, one of the Lofoten Islands, cod are still hung out to dry on wooden racks.

and sheep. The people lived in large, barnlike houses about 40 by 13 feet (12 by 4 meters). Large posts supported rafters carrying a roof made of straw and turf. There was a central fireplace for warmth and cooking, and during the long winters the animals were kept behind a partition at one end. In more northerly areas the farms were isolated, while in the south they were often grouped into villages. This pattern is still noticeable today.

The Scandinavians who lived on the coast fished, especially for herrings, which they smoked and salted for eating in winter. They became good boat builders able to make ships up to 78 feet (24 meters) long, a tremendous size for those days. They were the largest ships anyone had ever built. Cargo ships for the Baltic were wide with low sides, while ships for the rough Atlantic seas had higher sides. In 1983, a replica ship sailed the Atlantic in four weeks, almost reaching speeds attained by modern yachts.

During the period up to 800, Scandinavians grew increasingly wealthy. They were skilled at weaving cloth and making weapons, jewelry, and metal tools. The cloth was woven from their sheep but finer wool was imported from the Netherlands. Silk and gold thread for decoration were brought back by Scandinavians traveling into Russia. Their clothes were also decorated with jewelry worked in intricate patterns. Gold and silver were imported from Arabia as coins, melted down and worked into jewelry. Their skilled metalworkers also developed a wide range of weapons.

There have been many finds of costly jewelry and richly decorated bridles, helmets, swords, and shields. The weapons and buried hoards of coins suggest that many small-scale battles were fought as tribes spread and came into conflict with each other. Many of the local chieftains would have not only been farmers, but would have needed to be good swordsmen and warriors, too.

The men from the creeks

From among these warrior chiefs, their sons, and their slaves came the Viking raiders. Some may have been men for whom there was not enough land to farm. Others were probably warriors who had heard tales about the wealth of countries to the south and wished to fight for fortune and fame. Whatever the reason, between about A.D. 79 and 870, Viking longships sailed up the rivers of France, Britain, and the Netherlands. They

It was from narrow, steep-sided fjords or creeks, like this one at Sunndalsøra, that Vikings set sail to explore the world. It was very difficult to move from fjord to fjord overland, so the main method of transportation was by boat.

attacked the wealthy farmers who were no match for them in fighting.

Later, the Vikings began to settle in different parts of Europe. In England, a whole area of the north was ruled by the Danes. It was called the Danelaw, or the land under Danish Law. There the Vikings founded new towns or took over old ones like York, known as Jorvik to the Vikings. English farmers were forced to pay a tax called the Danegeld, or Danish money.

By 1016, all of England was under the Danish rule of King Cnut, or Canute, and was part of a Viking empire that included the Faeroes, northern Scotland, the Scottish Isles, and the Isle of Man. The empire also included parts of Ireland, where the Vikings founded Dublin. At about this time, too, Christian missionaries began

---

Viking Names
The Vikings left a lasting memorial in British place-names. In 1086, about 40 percent of the place-names in northeast England were Viking.

"By," as on the end of Whitby and Appleby, is the Viking word for town. "Thwaite" is from the Scandinavian word for a paddock, *thveit*, and occurs in many place-names. Other northern English words based on Viking words are fell, meaning mountain, and dale, meaning valley, from *fjell* and *dal*.

In France, the Vikings were known as the North Men, the Normans, whose descendants would conquer England in 1066.

---

to convert the now-settled Vikings. As they accepted local customs, and married locally, the differences between them and the original community faded away.

Iceland, Greenland, and Vinland

The greatest Viking adventures were in the rough North Atlantic Ocean. According to tradition, three Vikings first landed in Iceland in 860. Ten years later, Norwegians fleeing from the cruel rule of King Harald Fairhair began to settle in Iceland, and within a hundred years, about 50,000 people were there. By 930 they had a parliament, called the Althing, of 32 chieftain priests. The Althing made laws and judged disputes. The Althing is still the Icelandic parliament and is the oldest in the world.

The Viking settlers in Iceland were quick to pick quarrels and take revenge. They also liked to tell stories aloud as sagas, or "sayings," which were later written down, and are still enjoyed. The most famous, Burned Njal's Saga, tells how a feud grew, murder by murder, until a whole family was burned to death in their home.

A common Viking punishment was to make a wrongdoer an outlaw. About 980, one outlaw, Eric the Red, sailed west and sighted a gray, rocky coast with patches of land where he thought people could live, and glacier-covered mountains in the distance. Eric then returned to Iceland. In order to get people to join him in settling the new land, he called it, with some exaggeration, Greenland. A few brave people followed Eric, and founded two settlements. Eventually, about 3,000 Vikings were living in Greenland, but by the end of the fifteenth century this Norse outpost had faded away.

About the year 1000, Eric the Red's son Leif sailed west from Greenland to investigate an earlier sighting of a wooded coast with low hills. He found the coast and called it Markland, or Woodland. Following the shore southward, he came to a warmer country where there were wild vines growing. Leif called it Vinland. Leif's Markland and Vinland are very probably Labrador and Newfoundland. This means that Leif and his Vikings were the first Europeans to land in America, 500 years before the more famous Christopher Columbus!

4

Changing Kingdoms, Growing Independence

Until 1905 Scandinavian history was about the struggle between the two richest countries, Denmark and Sweden, to maintain northerly empires. At first, Denmark was the more powerful. In 811, one of its early tribal kings established the Eider River, now in Germany, as Denmark's southern border. By 900, Denmark was a single kingdom, and in the following century ruled Norway as well as parts of England and Sweden. For the next 300 years there were endless wars and marriages between many little earldoms within these lands. However, by the end of the thirteenth century, the winners of these struggles had created the three separate kingdoms of Denmark, Norway, and Sweden.

Swedes started settling on the west coast of Finland in the twelfth century. As the Swedes spread eastward, the Novgorodians, or early Russians, fought against them until, in 1323, a border was established in Karelia, which is now part of the Soviet Union. Finland became part of Sweden and remained so for nearly 500 years. In Finland today, six percent of the population still speaks Swedish as a first language.

The Union of Kalmar
In 1397, marriages and plotting between the Scandinavian royal families joined together the

Kingdoms and Republics

- Today, Denmark is the oldest single kingdom in the world. More than 50 monarchs go back in unbroken succession to old King Gorm in 900.

- Early Scandinavian kings had names like Harald Bluetooth, Sweyn Forkbeard, and Eric the Very Good.

- Like Denmark, Norway and Sweden are still kingdoms today.

- Iceland was one of the world's first republics, and remained a republic until 1262 when it became part of Norway. It became a republic again in 1944.

- Finland was a province of Sweden, then Russia, and became a republic in 1918.

three kingdoms of Norway, Denmark, and Sweden. In the Union of Kalmar, as it was called, Denmark was the strongest.

Part of Denmark's power came from its position overlooking Øresund, the entrance to the Baltic Sea. By building fortresses at the narrow points of the sound, Denmark could keep enemy fleets from passing, and charge customs duty on trading ships. Kronborg was the most important fort, built at Helsingør where Øresund is only 2.5 miles (4 kilometers) wide. Cannon from the windswept Kronborg walls could threaten passing ships while customs men set off to inspect their cargoes.

The Union of Kalmar lasted over a century, but there were many squabbles that led to bitter wars between Denmark and Sweden. Finally,

The fortress of Kronborg overlooks the Øresund where ships entering and leaving the Baltic Sea are channeled through a narrow stretch of water. The Danes put taxes on all trading ships, which they controlled from Kronborg. Kronborg was the model for the castle of Elsinore in Shakespeare's play Hamlet.

Kronborg Customs
The Danes had a novel method of checking customs dues. If a customs officer thought a ship's captain was lying about the value of his cargo, the officer had the power to buy it there and then for what the captain said it was worth. The cargo was then sold, and if it was indeed worth more, the king took the profit

This magnificent crest is part of the stern decoration of the ship Vasa, *launched in 1628. It was part of the large fleet of ships built by King Gustavus II Adolphus. The* Vasa *was top-heavy and sank. The well-preserved wreck was raised in 1961 and is on exhibition in a Stockholm museum.*

Sweden's national hero, King Gustavus Vasa, drove out the Danes in 1521. Slowly, Sweden began to get richer and stronger than Denmark. One reason was Sweden's industries. At Falun in central Sweden, copper had been mined since the tenth century, and by the seventeenth century Stora Kopparberg, the Great Copper Mountain, supplied 3,000 tons of copper each year to all of Europe. Copper sales made the country rich.

There was also a large iron industry in Sweden, and in the seventeenth century King Gustavus II Adolphus could afford to build a powerful naval fleet to invade the German states during the Thirty Years' War (1618–1648). Huge numbers of oak trees were cut down in Sweden's central provinces to build the ships.

Sweden flourishes

By the eighteenth century, Sweden was rich enough for its nobles to build grand summer houses and palaces. Drottingholm, the royal summer palace, is particularly beautiful. The king kept his own company of actors and singers at the palace, and brought famous composers, writers, and singers to perform in a deliberate attempt to show that Scandinavia could be as cultured as the rest of Europe.

In the early nineteenth century, the Scandinavians fought in the Napoleonic wars. Although they had tried to remain neutral and keep out of the wars, when the British attacked the Danish fleet and bombarded Copenhagen, Denmark sided with France's Napoleon. Russia defeated the Swedish armies in Finland and took over that country in 1809.

A group of Swedish noblemen and army officers were exasperated by the way King Gustavus IV had led the war, and forced him to give up the throne and go into exile. Sweden became a constitutional monarchy, and parliament looked for a new king. When Sweden made peace with Napoleon, one of his marshals, Count Bernadotte, was invited to found a new royal line. Finally, Denmark surrendered, and by the peace treaty of 1814 gave Norway to Sweden, keeping Iceland and the Faeroes.

The Industrial Revolution came late to Scandinavia, but by the end of the nineteenth century several large industries had been set up. Shipbuilding in Norway, iron ore from Swedish Lappland, and the growing export of wood pulp and paper instead of trees all helped the region.

During the seventeenth, eighteenth, and early nineteenth centuries Sweden was a powerful nation and played an important part in European history. The magnificent buildings on the waterfront in the capital, Stockholm, reflect the nation's wealth and the importance of the sea in Sweden's history.

Independence and nationalism

During the nineteenth century there were popular protests demanding the vote for all adults. However, these campaigns did not swell into revolutions as in other parts of Europe. Instead, there was a growing sense of national pride. In 1874, Iceland celebrated a thousand years of settlement by gaining home rule under its own parliament, the Althing. A similar, growing nationalism led Norway to declare itself independent of Sweden in 1905. However, Norway kept a royal family, and a Danish prince became Norway's King Haakon VII.

For the Finns, nationalism meant that by the end of the nineteenth century they could use their own language as well as Swedish for official business. However, Finland was split between those who supported the Russians and those who wanted independence. As World War I ended in 1918, the Finns took advantage of Russia's struggle against Germany to fight and win Finland's own independence.

The world wars

Scandinavian policy during World War I had been to stay neutral. The same policy failed in World War II. Russia conquered Finland when it refused to give Stalin the bases he needed against Germany. Hitler's armies overran Denmark and then Norway. However, to keep up the appearance of self-government, some Danes and Norwegians worked with the Germans. Sweden remained neutral, but allowed German troop movements through its territory and supplied Germany with large quantities of iron ore and vital ball-bearings. Nevertheless, Sweden became a haven for Norwegian and Danish Jews wanting to avoid Hitler's gas chambers.

As the war wore on, resistance movements grew in Denmark and Norway, putting out secret newspapers and blowing up troop trains and other targets. Their work is celebrated by Resistance Museums in Copenhagen and Oslo.

Norway and Finland probably suffered most from the war. Hitler's retreating armies burned many towns and farmhouses in northern Norway, which all had to be rebuilt. Finland had to pay the Soviet Union large amounts of compensation and give up ten percent of its territory. As a result, 400,000 Finns had to be resettled in other areas.

During World War II, some Scandinavian countries were occupied by Germany or the Soviet Union. Many buildings were badly damaged and after the war a massive rebuilding program was required. As a result, towns like Tapiola, near Helsinki, are good examples of modern city planning.

Since World War II, Norway, Denmark, and Iceland have become members of the North Atlantic Treaty Organization. NATO is the grouping of countries (including the United States and Britain) intended to balance the perceived threat from the Soviet Union and Eastern Europe. Finland has maintained its independence by balancing its policies so as to upset neither the Soviet Union nor the West. Sweden's prosperity owes much to its wartime neutrality. Other countries could learn from the way Scandinavia benefits because of comparatively low spending on armed forces.

5 Travel Within Scandinavia and Beyond

Towns and villages are spread thinly across Scandinavia and are rarely far from water. Since so much of the countryside is mountainous or covered in dense forest, seas, rivers, and lakes have always offered the best way to travel. Boat travel is as much part of Scandinavian life as car travel in other countries.

Shipping

Scandinavians soon saw the value of the early steam engines, and started using coastal steamers in 1838. The arrival of the little ship carrying parcels and news became an important event in the lives of far-flung townships. Today, a regular service runs the 1,250 miles (2,000 kilometers) along Norway's coast from Bergen, across the Arctic Circle, past the Lofoten Islands and the North Cape, around to Kirkenes on the Russian border.

Along most Scandinavian coastlines, hundreds of small ships and hydrofoils run frequent services between the mainland and the many small islands. Regular ferries cross Norway's fjords and link Denmark's islands, large and small. Ferries also create an easy link between Denmark and Sweden. Trains run straight onto the ferry at Helsingør, and a half hour later are on Swedish rails at Helsingborg.

Ferries travel all around the Baltic Sea throughout the year, although during the winter the seas are often full of ice floes. These ships in Helsinki harbor carry some of the eight million passengers crossing between Stockholm and Helsinki each year.

Very large ferries also carry eight million people every year between Stockholm and Helsinki.

The Scandinavians also keep large trading fleets. The Norwegians have often acted as carriers for other nation's goods. Today, although smaller than in the 1960s, Norway's merchant fleet is still an important source of that country's income.

Traveling by snow and ice

In winter, frozen lakes and bays make a convenient shortcut. In earlier days, they also used to offer a much better way of moving heavy goods than using rough and hilly roads. The loads were put on sledges and pulled across the ice. Horses were used in the south and reindeer in the north. As recently as the 1950s, before Finland built modern roads, it was easier for cars to travel along frozen rivers.

Railroads

Much of the Scandinavian Peninsula is a railroad builder's nightmare, needing many expensive tunnels and bridges. At the same time, the scattered population means there are few people to buy tickets. As a result, railroads have been slow to develop.

In large cities like Oslo, streetcars are a popular method of transportation because they are generally able to run safely whatever the weather conditions.

Oslo-Bergen Railroad

The most difficult railroad to build in Scandinavia was the spectacular line between Oslo and the major western port of Bergen in Norway. On a map, the two cities are only 190 miles (300 kilometers) apart, but in reality they are separated by the Hardanger mountain range, which is snowbound throughout the year and capped by a glacier. Originally, the only way to travel between Bergen and Oslo was around the southern tip of Norway, a tedious four-day journey by stagecoach, or three days by boat.

The Bergen to Oslo railroad was suggested in 1870 and had to be built by the government. Surveying took five years; during this time weather stations were set up to find the route with least snowfall. Unhappily, they found that snow fell on the mountains in every month of the year, with an average winter depth of 13 feet (four meters). The line had to climb steeply, and in 47 mountainous miles (75 kilometers), the contractors had to build 11 miles (18 kilometers) of tunnels. Much of the time, the tunnels were bored through hard granite rock and, not surprisingly, the project took 30 years to complete. Steam trains cut the journey time to 14 hours, while today's electric trains take only seven hours. Nevertheless, it is a hard route to keep open, with frequent rockfalls and snowdrifts. On the high part of the line near the glacier, the line runs through almost continuous snowsheds, which are a kind of wooden tunnel.

One of the most important railroad lines in Scandinavia runs northwest over the Norwegian frontier from the Swedish iron-ore mines at

Kiruna and Gällivare to the port of Narvik. At Narvik there is one of the largest ore-handling terminals in Europe, and the railroad means that Sweden can export iron ore even when the Baltic is frozen. Sweden is also famous for having the first railroad bridge built of steel. It was opened in 1866 and spanned the Trolhätten Gorge in southern Sweden.

The steep-sided fjords often make road building difficult and, because it is not easy to find a short route, distances between villages such as Okesandalsøra and other places are often very long.

Road travel

It is only recently that Scandinavian roads have reached anything like the standard of those in other European countries. In the mountains, roads twist and turn to gain height, while the many rivers and lakes mean long detours. Winter snow and ice make mountain roads impassable,

and studded snow tires soon wear out the road surface. As a result, road travel until the 1960s was slow and inconvenient.

Since then, Scandinavian prosperity has led to many improvements. There are fleets of snowplows that come out the instant snow falls to keep the roads open. Denmark has a good network of highways for its size and there are fast new roads in southern Norway and Sweden. As part of a deliberate plan to improve conditions in northern Norway, a huge government program of tunneling and fjord-bridging has made the road to the North Cape an engineering masterpiece. Many small ferries have been replaced by bridges, cutting travel times considerably.

Air travel
The mountainous terrain and the long distances involved make air travel important to Norway and Sweden. There are many airports for flights within the countries, and frequent services even to quite small towns.

Once Iceland could only be reached by a rough three- or four-day sea journey from Denmark or Norway. Modern air travel now means that Icelanders no longer feel so cut off from the rest of the Scandinavian countries.

Iceland has its own small airline, Icelandair; Finland's airline, Finnair, is considerably larger. Denmark, Norway, and Sweden have joined together to create one large airline, Scandinavian Airlines System. SAS prides itself on serving the business traveler well, and has no trouble keeping its aircraft full.

Polar explorers

The experience of Norwegians in living and hunting in the cold north gives them an advantage in polar exploration. Svalbard, the Spitzbergen islands, were surveyed for minerals in 1827, while in 1888 the scientist and explorer Fridtjof Nansen crossed Greenland, reaching a height of 9,000 feet (2,700 meters). Later Nansen had a specially strengthened boat, the *Fram*, built to test his theories of a polar current. The *Fram* was allowed to become fixed in drifting ice off Russia's New Siberian Islands. Rather than being crushed, the *Fram's* hull allowed it to ride up over the ice, and three years later the boat emerged as predicted near Spitzbergen. Nansen meanwhile had tried to reach the North Pole on dogsleds, and came closer than any other explorer had done before.

In 1911, the Norwegian explorer Roald Amundsen sailed in the *Fram*, intending to cross Antarctica and reach the South Pole. The British Captain Robert F. Scott had the same plan. Amundsen reached the Pole on December 14, a month before Scott, and returned successfully while Scott's polar party perished. The *Fram* is now kept in its own museum on Oslofjord.

6 A Living from Land and Sea

Historically, Denmark and the region of Skåne in southern Sweden were known as "the bread basket" of Scandinavia because this was where most of the grain was grown. Farther north, wheat and barley will only grow on the land around the warmer, sheltered fjords of Norway's western coast. Even there, summer comes late, and north-facing slopes stay cold until May. However, the long summer days make up for the short summer, and cereal crops can grow from seed to ripening in 90 days. Farmers gamble on harvesting as late as possible.

Most farms are somewhat isolated because the land available for farming is limited. Traditional wooden farm buildings like this house and barn in Sunndalsfjord can be found scattered along most fjords.

Traditionally, the climate has meant that the more northerly farmers have preferred to concentrate on sheep and cattle rearing. In the past, most animals were slaughtered in autumn and the meat was preserved in salt for winter food. Only a few breeding animals were kept for the spring. In the winter, farmers would also hunt reindeer and wildfowl for food.

This type of farming has resulted in the scatter of small isolated settlements that is so characteristic of Scandinavia. Along any valley bottom the road passes by small, separate farms. Many of the wooden buildings are still painted in the traditional colors: white for the farmhouse and dark brownish-red ("ox-blood") or dark green for the barns and cow-sheds.

Today, hay silos have become a common sight on northern farms, as well as in the greener south, and cheap imported animal food means that livestock can now be kept through the winter. In Iceland and the Faeroe Islands, the cold windy climate makes cattle rearing difficult, so sheep farming is vital to their economy.

The Danish example

Denmark has few mineral resources, so farming is immensely important to the economy. The warmer climate, similar to Oregon's, has made successful farming possible, and the rich, peaty land of central and eastern Denmark looks almost like one large vegetable garden.

Danish farming is very intensive and centers on dairy products and pig raising. Since the nineteenth century many Scandinavian farmers, but particularly the Danish, have formed

In Denmark, the soil is rich and the land is flatter than most other parts of Scandinavia. Farming is a major industry in Denmark, so the country has many farms, such as these around Amager near Copenhagen.

cooperatives. These meant that groups of farms could buy animal food and fertilizer in bulk and, therefore, at a better price. At the same time, each cooperative could afford to employ people to market the products of all its members. This was especially important for Denmark because of its need to earn money through exports.

Food for Scandinavia

Since World War II, Scandinavia's general prosperity has helped many farmers to pay for the equipment needed for modern farming. However, not all farms are highly mechanized and there is a wide range of farming methods, from high-tech dairy barns with milking machines in Denmark to traditional peasant farming in Scandinavia's far northwest. Modern

47

Only the bottom of the valleys are suitable for farming in western Norway. The high mountain slopes stay partially snow-covered through most of the year, but in the sheltered valleys farmers can grow a limited variety of vegetables and wheat or barley.

farming methods now mean that Denmark, Sweden, and even Norway are generally self-sufficient in basic foodstuffs.

Even so, the long, gloomy winters mean that, especially in the north, green vegetables and fruit become scarce and expensive. The produce sections of supermarkets in the smaller towns have a small selection over the winter months. Many Scandinavians take vitamin supplements in winter, and go wild with joy when fresh, home-grown vegetables return to the markets, and people feel they can "taste the summer."

Timber!
Huge areas of Scandinavia are covered in pine and fir trees. They are a major economic resource and have three main uses: for timber, for paper-

making, and for chemical products. The main chemicals are resins, tar-oils, and pitches, which can all be extracted from the trees. Products such as turpentine and Stockholm Tar (from pine trees) were once used in large quantities by painters and shipbuilders, but for the most part these chemicals have now been replaced by petroleum-based versions. Norwegian spruce trees used to be in great demand for the masts of sailing ships because of their height, strength, and the straightness of their trunks. The main use of spruce today is for building timber.

Sweden, Norway, and Finland have thousands of square miles of forest that are used as a major resource. The latest technology and equipment are utilized so that the timber can be felled and cut most economically.

Plywood is made from thin layers of birch glued together, and Finland is the world's leading exporter of this timber product. In addition, Finland is second only to Canada in exports of fiberboard and paper. Sweden exports huge

quantities of paper and woodpulp.

Large areas of forest are cut down each year for the paper industry, especially in Sweden and Finland. Much of the timber is taken out on trucks, but in remoter regions, rafts of logs are floated down the rivers and through the lakes to the pulping mills. Handling felled trees in these quantities is a skilled job, and the loggers, as the workers are called, often have to make dangerous leaps from log to log far out from shore to clear a logjam. Despite the large numbers of trees felled, replanting programs mean that Scandinavia should never lose its forests. However, they have one main threat—the acid rain blown in from other European countries, in particular Britain and Germany. This rain, which is a result of industrial pollution, can kill off the trees.

Besides being an important industry in Scandinavia, fishing on a smaller scale has made an important contribution to the tables of many families. Ice fishing by drilling through a frozen lake surface has been a method used for hundreds of years.

Fishing

Scandinavia's long coastlines make fishing an important industry. Historically, herring fishing off southern Sweden was an important addition to Skane's wealth. Overfishing has almost wiped out the herring, and the same is true in the North Sea. Cod, on the other hand, are still brought in quantity to the Lofoten Islands, and dried by traditional methods. The headless cod are hung on special wooden drying racks where the cold salt winds preserve the fish until they look like dried pieces of gray leather. Much of the dried cod is exported to Africa as a source of protein.

The Cod Wars

Iceland's lack of good farming land has made fishing a vital part of the country's economy, both in the past and today. When refrigerator ships were invented, Iceland's export trade in fish increased dramatically. Unfortunately, the rich fishing grounds around Iceland attract boats from many countries, Britain in particular. To protect its fishing industry, Iceland increased its offshore limits three times between 1959 and 1975, from 12 miles to 50 and then to 200 (19 kilometers to 80 to 320). Only Icelandic boats could fish in these waters. Britain disputed the claim, and this led to a series of encounters in which Icelandic and British naval boats bumped each other and their rival fishing boats.

The Cod Wars, as they were called, resulted in Britain acknowledging Iceland's claim. They also emphasized the Scandinavians' determination to make the most of their resources.

7 Lego, Steel, and White Coal

Some industries, such as mining and shipbuilding, have a long history in Scandinavia. Others, such as the hydroelectric and oil and gas industries, are more recent. Today, Scandinavia's wealth of power and minerals, and the high quality of its products, combine to give most of its people a very high standard of living.

Mining

Early miners roamed over Sweden's central mountains, no doubt hoping to find another huge deposit of copper like that found at Stora Kopparberg. Instead, they discovered workable deposits of iron ore in the Bergslagen district, where the town of Nora became the industry's center. In the nineteenth century, the area was dotted with iron-smelting works and manor houses, such as Siggebohyttan, built by the newly rich ironmasters.

Today, Sweden mines well over 20 million tons of iron ore a year, about ten percent of world production. The Swedish state owns the largest mine at Kiruna, well north of the Arctic Circle, and 5,000-ton trains take the ore over the Ofoten railway to the ice-free Norwegian port of Narvik for shipment.

Steel

In Norway, the only large steelworks is the state-owned plant at Mo I Rana, almost on the Arctic

Circle. The iron is mined in Dunderlandsdal and brought by rail to one of the world's largest iron-smelting furnaces. Norway also has a specialist industry producing alloys of steel. Scandinavia lacks the coal needed to turn its ore into iron. The only important coal mines are on Svalbard, the island group halfway between the North Cape and the North Pole, where Norway removes 600,000 tons of coal each year. What a test of endurance it must be, to dig out coal in the cold and dark polar winter!

Norway, Sweden, and Finland mine sizeable quantities of zinc and lead, while Finland mines 24,000 tons of copper each year, a little more than

The steel hull of a new ship being built at Turku in Finland. The Finns concentrate on building specialist ships such as icebreakers.

Norway. The mine at Outokumpu in Finland is the largest copper mine in Europe, although reserves are dwindling. Finland also produces a ton of gold each year. Other rare minerals may well be discovered in the more remote north. It is known that Sweden holds 15 percent of world reserves of uranium.

Other industries

Shipbuilding has long been important for all the Nordic countries except Iceland. In the 1970s, Scandinavia as a whole had the biggest merchant fleet in the world. Recent Japanese and North Korean competition has caused a decline in both shipping and shipbuilding. Luckily, Norwegian shipyards have been able to turn to building oil rigs for the North Sea, while Finland has begun making ice-breaking and other specialist ships. Finland is also an important manufacturer of paper-making machinery.

Sweden has also built up a car industry, which now emphasizes quality and safety. Volvo and Saab cars are sold all over the world, and in Scandinavia every second car seems to be one of these two makes.

In comparison to these heavy industries, Denmark's industries seem lighthearted. It has enormous breweries making and exporting beer; and Lego, the children's construction toy, also comes from Denmark. However, since World War II, Denmark has also developed its food-processing industries, and builds bridges overseas with the knowledge it has gained from linking Jylland with the island of Fyn and Sjaelland with Falster.

Legoland near Billund, Denmark, is a major tourist attraction. The entire theme park is constructed from the small plastic bricks and other pieces that make up this Danish-made, internationally popular toy.

Power

With hardly any coal, but many mountain rivers, the invention of hydroelectric power was a blessing to Norway, Sweden, and Iceland. Norway, in particular, has built enormous electricity-generating stations, powered by water rushing down from high lakes. Production of electricity from water power is almost pollution-free, and the turbines that generate the electricity are often housed underground. People call hydroelectricity "white coal."

Norway has used its immense supplies of hydroelectricity to produce fertilizers and aluminum. These processes are the basis of the huge Norsk Hydro company. It is the world's largest producer of artificial fertilizers, with an annual output of 12 million tons. The Hydro aluminum division makes 620,000 tons per year, overshadowing steel production and putting Norway in the top league of aluminum producers.

In Iceland, besides hydroelectricity, there is another cheap, inexhaustible energy source— geothermal energy. This is energy from the heat in the Earth's rocks. The heat warms up the water of the geysers or hot springs for which the island is famous; these are tapped and their hot water is piped to warm people's homes.

Although Finland has so many lakes, it is generally too flat for much hydroelectricity to be generated. In recent years, Finland has bought

Water cascading down the many mountains in Norway and Sweden provides an unlimited source of hydroelectric power. This power plant at Aura is one of a major network.

nuclear reactors from the Soviet Union as well as oil and natural gas, which are piped overland. Even Sweden has had to build nuclear power stations. However, as a result of a 1980 vote, Sweden has decided to phase out its 12 nuclear reactors by the year 2010. Finland is building coal- and peat-fired power stations instead of a fifth nuclear reactor.

North Sea oil and gas

The development of the North Sea oil and gas industry since the 1970s has been essential for Denmark's development, because, like Finland, it has few other energy sources. In 1973, Denmark had to import 95 percent of the petroleum it needed, but by 1987 this figure was down to 48 percent. In the 1990s, Denmark's oil and gas

Oil and natural gas from the North Sea are now a major source of energy in Scandinavia. Giant oil rigs were built in the shipyards at Oslo and pulled out to sea.

production should meet more than 70 percent of its needs.

Norway has found North Sea oil and gas a valuable bonus and is now one of the world's top ten oil producers. Frigg, Ekofisk, and Stadtjord are the main fields, and they produce far more than Norway needs, so it exports oil and gas to other West European countries. For example, every day the Heimdal rig pumps 10.5 to 13 million cubic yards (8 to 10 million cubic meters) of methane gas through two undersea pipelines to reach Emden in Germany, 375 miles (600 kilometers) to the south. The rig is out in the North Sea 63 miles (100 kilometers) west of Stavanger.

Life on the North Sea oil rigs is hard, particularly in the stormy winter cold, but the work pays well. Shifts are 12 hours long, and both men and women work two weeks nonstop before having three weeks off. Space is cramped, and being able to get along well with fellow workers is one of the most important job qualifications. The Norwegians have insisted on high safety standards, and there have been far fewer casualties than there have been on British rigs. The Norwegian platforms have free-fall lifeboats, and a rescue ship on standby that crew members call "our watchdog."

The income from oil and gas makes up 42 percent of all Norway's export earnings. As a result, when world oil prices drop, Norway gets into financial difficulties. Since the North Sea reserves will eventually run out, the hardy Norwegians plan to drill much farther north, in the Arctic waters of the Barents Sea.

Inventions and discoveries

Resourceful Scandinavians have invented and developed a variety of products, many of which have led to the growth of important industries.

In the 1880s, the Swedish scientist Arrhenius first had the ideas that led to electrolysis, the separation of metals using an electric current.

The Nobel Prize

When the inventor Alfred Nobel died, he wrote in his will that a large part of his fortune should be used to set up a fund for special awards. Today, Nobel Prizes are an important recognition for top scientists, writers, and peace workers.

Winners of the Nobel Prize include:

1903, 1911 Marie Curie, France (for discovering radium)

1921 Albert Einstein, Germany (for theoretical physics)

1922 Niels Bohr, Denmark (for investigating atomic structure)

1945 Sir Alexander Fleming, Britain (for discovering penicillin)

1953 Sir Winston Churchill, Britain (for descriptive writing and speech) Francis Crick, Britain, James Watson, U.S., and Maurice Wilkins, Britain (for working out how DNA enables life to reproduce)

1962 John Steinbeck, U.S. (for realistic and imaginative writing)

1964 Martin Luther King, Jr., U.S. (for peace)

1965 Mikhail Sholokhov, Soviet Union (for his epic novels)

1979 Mother Teresa, India (for peace)

1983 Lech Walesa, Poland (for peace)

This process became very valuable when Scandinavia developed cheap hydroelectricity, as the countries could then produce aluminum more cheaply than other parts of the world.

The safety heads on matches were invented in Stockholm in 1846, and in 1892 Alexander Lagerman, also from Sweden, invented a machine for making the huge quantity of 100,000 matches an hour. C.D. Ekman invented a process for making the valuable raw material, cellulose, from wood-chippings in the 1870s.

The most important nineteenth-century inventor in Scandinavia was Alfred Nobel, who made a fortune from explosives. In particular, he found a way of making the dangerous chemical nitroglycerine safe to handle. Dynamite, as he called his invention, immediately replaced gunpowder for rock blasting. Nobel set up factories for making explosives in France, Germany, and Britain, and these plants have made huge profits from the wars of the last 100 years.

8   City Life

All the major Scandinavian cities are ports, with all their characteristic bustle and activity. Often the city center seems to be built on the waterfront, giving a sense of space and light, while the moored ships suggest escape and adventure overseas. The cities have the advantage of not being too large. Copenhagen is the biggest with a population of only 1.4 million, yet it has a compact center. Almost all the other cities are hilly, with trees separating the valley suburbs.

The waterways of Inner Nyhaven, Copenhagen, are like streets, with boats traveling alongside the pedestrians and vehicles.

Although the population is concentrated in these coastal cities, they do not feel overcrowded and jammed with traffic as do many cities in other parts of the world. Pollution from local industries

is not as big a problem as in many countries, and the Scandinavian city centers have not been destroyed by road building. Even so, they are not old-fashioned, although quaint old streets can be found. Rather, the Scandinavian capital cities have a pleasing mixture of old and new.

Denmark's capital, Copenhagen

In Danish the city's name is Køpenhavn, which means the merchants' port, and waterways still push into its very center. When the Knippel bridge lifts up to let a large liner glide out into the Øresund, car drivers stuck in the traffic jams have to accept that shipping rules the city. Even the Little Mermaid, the sculpture that has become Denmark's tourist symbol, is set between a park and a shipbuilder's yard.

The center of Copenhagen has been turned into a pedestrian zone, and in summer its narrow streets and open squares are full of little stands selling all kinds of jewelry and knickknacks. Beyond the zone are wide streets of chic shops, and the Tivoli gardens. The Tivoli is an amusement park in the heart of Copenhagen. There are fairground rides, restaurants, and an outdoor theater, as well as flower gardens that are lit up at dusk for evening strolls. With the Tivoli, Copenhagen seems to be a city made for fun and enjoyment. Copenhagen does not have the slightly stern appearance of the other Scandinavian capitals, perhaps because it lies to the south of the region.

None of Denmark's other cities is nearly as large as Copenhagen. Århus, the next largest, has a population of only 194,000.

Helsinki is famous for its modern buildings, in particular the Finlandia concert hall, which overlooks Töölö Bay in the heart of the city.

Finland's capital, Helsinki

Helsinki, Finland's capital city, has a small compact center with wide streets and modern, covered shopping malls. The original wooden town was destroyed repeatedly by great fires. Today, it is a city of apartment and public buildings in modern architectural styles. The Finlandia concert hall is particularly impressive as it overlooks Töölö Bay.

The old city center is Senate Square. This square was begun in 1812 when the Russians moved the Finnish capital closer to them, from Turku to Helsinki. Surrounding three sides of the square are the university, cathedral, and government palace. They are all built of stone in the harmonious if rather severe style called "neo-classical." Helsinki is said to be the last European city that was "designed as a whole and created as a work of art."

Central Helsinki is almost an island. The people who live there call it "an apple hanging from a tree." Narrow arms of water point into the center, making useful natural harbors. Helsinki sprawls northward on the mainland, and with its 488,000 inhabitants is three times larger than Finland's other main cities: Tampere, Turku, Espoo, and Vantaa. Their populations range in order from 170,000 down to 149,000.

Iceland's capital, Reykjavik

Reykjavik, with just over 90,000 inhabitants, is by far the smallest of all the Scandinavian capitals, yet half of Iceland's population lives in the city and its surrounding areas. The story of Reykjavik's founding is told in the Icelandic sagas. In 874, Ingolfur Arnarson was sailing in the North Atlantic, and followed the old Viking custom to choose his destination. He took the carved posts that stood on either side of his "head-of-family" chair and threw them into the sea, saying "I will settle where they are washed up." The site of his homestead is now covered by the center of Reykjavik.

The city has a tiny center with two main harbors. The Parliament building, opera house, theaters, art galleries, and Nordic House cultural center are all within easy walking distance. Iceland is trying to develop Reykjavik, and indeed the whole island, as a tourist attraction in order to earn money. Besides being used for heating homes, Iceland's hot springs heat open-

The main thoroughfare in Iceland's small capital city is much less grand than those of other Scandinavian capitals. However, it still has all the facilities for urban life.

air swimming pools in Reykjavik and elsewhere. The tourist brochures boast that Iceland, of all places, is the only country where it is pleasant to swim outdoors in the middle of winter.

Norway's capital, Oslo

Oslo, Norway's capital city, sits back from the Oslofjord. At the center, in the wide Karl Johans Gate, the waterside is forgotten in a way it never is in Copenhagen, Helsinki, or Stockholm. *"Gate"* and *"gata"* are words for "street," and Karl Johans Gate is Oslo's main street. It runs from the Royal Palace in the west, past the National Theater, the university, and the Parliament building, to end at the Central Station in the east.

A little south of Karl Johans Gate is Oslo's large, modern city hall overlooking the Oslofjord. There are good ferry services from here, in particular to some of Oslo's many museums on the peninsula of Bygdøy. In their own museum, the preserved Viking ships are breathtaking in their sheer size and clear, sweeping lines. Nearby, Nansen's ship *Fram* is preserved as are Thor Heyerdahl's rafts *Kon-Tiki* and *Ra II*, on which he crossed the Pacific and Atlantic oceans to show the long sea migrations ancient peoples could have made. Traditional Scandinavian buildings have been reconstructed nearby.

Frognor Park is the home of a vast outdoor collection of statues by Gustav Vigeland. Above the park the hills start, and a little tramway crowded at rush hour winds up through wealthy suburbs and pine-clad slopes to Holmenkøllen, where there is the largest ski jump in the world. Skiing is very much part of life in Oslo, where there are 60 miles (96 kilometers) of ski trails within the city limits.

Bergen, Norway's second largest city, is on the west coast. Its old wooden buildings are a reminder of the times when it was an important port, with trade run by German merchants of the Hanseatic League, an association of medieval German cities. While Oslo is a bright, thriving

Oslo boasts the largest ski jump in the world, the Holmenkøllen. A huge amphitheater at the base of the jump is filled regularly with spectators for this exciting sport.

city, Bergen, with its mists and frequent rain, seems like a memento of old Scandinavia. Norway also has the world's most northerly town, Hammerfest.

Sweden's capital, Stockholm

Medieval Stockholm was built on a small island where Lake Mälaren flows into the Baltic Sea. Today, Stockholm is a large modern city of 667,000 people. The city is spread over 14 islands. The buildings are solidly made, often of bright red brick with green copper roofs. For the tourist, there are plenty of museums, galleries, and

The Old Town of Stockholm has narrow cobbled streets.

interesting sights. The Old Town still stands, with its thirteenth-century cathedral and the more recent royal palace. Nearby are the locks and weirs that let water out of Lake Mälaren and let boats onto the lake.

With the city's many bays and channels, water is always close at hand, and its modern city hall, like Oslo's, looks directly over the water. From the city hall, boats take sightseers out to the royal palace at Drotingholm and other lakeside attractions, such as Gripsholm Castle at Mariefred. On the other side of the Old Town, boats leave for trips around some of the 200,000 islands along Stockholm's coastline. Many of the city dwellers have second homes on one of the islands, giving them a weekend and vacation escape for swimming and fishing.

Sweden's next largest cities, Gothenburg (Göteborg in Swedish) and Malmö, have populations of 432,000 and 231,000, respectively. Both are important modern ports; Gothenburg, which has many islands nearby, is also popular with vacationers.

9   The Nordic People

The sharply contrasting seasons have a strong effect on Scandinavian life-styles. Above all, Scandinavians have learned to be practical, whether in shoveling deep snow off the roof in winter, or enjoying a cool drink on a late summer evening, with mosquito repellent burning in the clear, sharp air.

Homes

These houses in Vadstena, Sweden, are built in the traditional way, with brightly painted timber. They are well insulated against the winter cold.

Scandinavian homes are well adapted to winter. Old wooden houses may still have an iron or porcelain stove that stands out into the room, while modern houses and apartments have central heating. One of the advantages that

countries with high snowfalls have is that the snow that lies thick on the roof and drifts against the walls acts as additional insulation, keeping the heat inside.

Nearly all the windows in Scandinavian buildings are double- or triple-glazed. The space between the outer double-glazed window and the inner single pane is often decorated with pretty ornaments to catch what little sunlight there is. Inside, plants crowd against the windows so that there is greenery when everything outside seems black and white.

The tradition of painting wooden houses a bold color like dark green, red, or yellow, has been continued on modern buildings. Often, though, pastel shades replace the older colors. Scandinavian towns look bright and cheerful on all but the most dismal of winter days.

Food

The closeness of the sea means there are many different fish dishes. Salmon is a common but expensive ingredient, while some dishes, such as *surströmming*, or fermented herring, seem strange to tourists. Crab and crayfish feasts are a treat in late summer.

In Finland, reindeer is eaten stewed or roasted, but because reindeer is expensive, beef, pork, and lots of potato dishes are more common. Traditional dishes in Sweden include herring or meatballs and, for special occasions, the *smörgàsbord*, or cold table. In Denmark and Norway there are elaborate open sandwiches called *smørrebrød*, or "buttered bread." Sometimes the bread is barely visible beneath a

A selection of vegetables can be bought in Helsinki, Finland, but most of them are imported except during the summer months.

delicious mound of cheese or meat!

For breakfast, Scandinavians traditionally eat thin slices of sausage or cheese on bread. In Norway, the cheese is usually made from goats' milk. Today, people are just as likely to eat cereal. Thin Scandinavian crispbread made from rye is now sold all over the world, but in Scandinavia it can be bought as huge circular crackers in boxes.

Scandinavian languages

The Norwegian, Swedish, and Danish languages are very similar. People from these three countries can understand each other without too much difficulty. The reason for this is the close historical links between the countries. Indeed, while Norway was under Danish rule, Danish was the official language for courts, parliament, and business. Norwegian children were taught in Danish, and Norwegian existed as a spoken rather than a written language.

As Norwegians began their move toward independence during the nineteenth century, many of them, and in particular Ivar Åasen, set about creating a new language, a language of the people, based on dialects spoken in districts far away from Danish influence. This became known as either Landsmål, the language of the land, or Nynorsk, New Norwegian.

Another set of reformers adapted Danish to the Norwegian spoken in the southeast, closest to Denmark. Known as Riksmål or Bokmål, the State or Book Language, this was used by the playwright Ibsen and a number of poets. The two languages differ very little, and educated Norwegians understand both.

Norwegian, Swedish, and Danish are Germanic languages and have a large number of

Comparison of Scandinavian Words with English Ones. (Note: g and j often sound like y as in yes)

Danish	Norwegian	Swedish	English
dag	dag	dag	day
datter	datter	dotter	daughter
drink	drikk	drink	drink
nat	natt	natt	night
god	god	god	good
tak!	takk!	tack!	thanks!
told	toll	tull	toll (i.e. customs)
øl	øl	öl	ale (i.e. beer)
rødvin	rødvin	rödvin	red wine
maelk	melk	mjölk	milk

words that are similar to German. As a result of Viking rule in Britain, the Scandinavian languages have given many words to English.

Of all the Scandinavian languages, Icelandic has changed least, and is still close to the language used in the old Icelandic sagas. Indeed, it is not difficult for modern Icelanders to read these ancient prose narratives written in the original version.

Finnish is quite separate from the other Scandinavian languages because a different group of people settled there originally. The closest modern language to Finnish, as might be expected, is the one spoken in the Estonian republic of the Soviet Union, across the narrow Gulf of Finland. Finnish is also related to Hungarian, and this small group of languages is called the Finno-Ugric group. The language of the Saami is part of the same group, although curiously, Finns find it easier to understand Estonians than the Saami.

Immigrants and emigrants
The historic links between the Scandinavian countries mean that there has been a considerable movement of people among them. In particular, there are quite large Finnish minorities in Norway and Sweden. None of the countries has had large overseas empires, so there has been relatively little immigration from outside Scandinavia. Caribbeans, Indian Asians, and Arabic peoples are rarely seen. There are, however, sizable Asian minorities, especially since most Scandinavian countries have welcomed people who have felt oppressed in their native lands. Quite a large

number of Vietnamese, for example, have come to Denmark and Sweden recently.

Emigration is another story. The poverty of much of Scandinavia in the nineteenth century led many people to leave their countries. Sweden lost about 20 percent of its population to the United States. Twentieth-century prosperity has slowed the pace of emigration.

Government

All five Scandinavian countries are democracies, meaning that they are governed by parliaments elected by the votes of adults, both men and women. Denmark, Norway, and Sweden are also monarchies. In practice, the king or queen is not involved in everyday politics and in many ways is little more than a figurehead. Real power is in the hands of a prime minister and cabinets drawn from elected members of parliament.

Finland and Iceland are both republics, with presidents who are elected by the vote of the whole adult population. The Finnish president has more power, like the president of the United States, while Iceland's president tends to be more of a figurehead.

Typically in Scandinavian politics there are many relatively small parties, ranging from Communists to extreme right-wing groups. To form a government, the parties often have to join together in larger groups or coalitions. On the whole, Scandinavians have voted for left-of-center rather than right-wing parties. The Labor Party in Norway and the Social Democrats in Denmark, Sweden, and Finland have most often been the main parties in power.

The systems of local government vary considerably from country to country. Finland has 12 provinces, each with a governor. In Sweden, which is divided into regions that are divided in turn into provinces, local councils have more power than in the other countries.

In Scandinavia there is great respect for individual rights. Partly this has evolved because of the idea, started in Sweden in 1800, of the ombudsman. This official provides a free service to any person who has a complaint about the way various government departments work. The ombudsman's duty is to investigate the complaint. This usually solves the problem. Other countries are now adopting this idea.

Arts and crafts

It is really only since the middle of the nineteenth century that Scandinavia has made important contributions to the worlds of painting, music, and literature. By far the best-known artist is Norway's Edvard Munch. Born in 1863, his

Carl Larsson (1853–1919) was a Swedish painter. His delightful paintings of everyday life in Sweden, such as Emma's Birthday, *painted in 1900, are becoming increasingly popular.*

The monument to Sibelius, Finland's most famous composer, stands in a park in Helsinki. It captures the wintry grandeur of Sibelius's music.

greatest works were painted in the first 20 years of this century. He had an immense body of work covering a wide range of subjects, from factory workers to family groups. He was good at depicting emotions such as jealousy and grief.

In music, the majestic harmonies of Finland's Jean Sibelius contrast with the more lyrical sounds of Norway's Edvard Grieg. Grieg is perhaps best known for the *Peer Gynt Suite*. This orchestral piece was written to accompany Henrik Ibsen's play *Peer Gynt*. Ibsen, who died in 1906, is Norway's major playwright. His most famous plays attacked the narrow-mindedness of small-town life. Ibsen is rivaled by Sweden's August Strindberg, whose plays used symbolic characters to express emotional states.

There have been comparatively few Scandinavian novelists, although Norway's Knut Hamsun has become widely known. The writer who has gained the most international fame is of course Denmark's Hans Christian Andersen. His children's stories have been translated into most of the world's languages. In recent years, the Finnish writer Tove Jansson has become well known for the Moomintroll children's books.

In the film world, Sweden's Ingmar Bergman is an internationally recognized director. In radio and television, the similarity of the languages makes it easy for Scandinavians to cooperate and produce joint programs, but this is also a barrier to the rest of Europe.

Where Scandinavians have had an immense worldwide influence is in design. The Finnish architect Alvar Aalto is renowned for using concrete and glass to make elegantly functional buildings. Aalto influenced furniture design in the same way, along with his pupil, the Danish Arne Jacobsen. They and many others have made Danish interior design world-famous for a clear-cut line that does away with fussy clutter and decoration. This influence has spread to tableware. Sweden and Finland are world leaders in elegant glassware.

Throughout the world, clean lines, the use of light, unstained wood, and neat, simple furnishings can all be attributed to Scandinavian influence. Although the Nordic people may not have been strong in the fine arts, they have excelled at stylish design for everyday living.

10 Religion

The Vikings had a range of gods who could be called upon to suit different occasions and a great wealth of stories about them. The one with greatest power was Odin, god of poetry and master of magic, who could hear the grass grow. Thor, god of thunder, was very strong physically. He carried a huge hammer, named Mjollnir, and hammer symbols are often found on Viking jewelry. Frejya was the goddess of love. All three gods' names are remembered in the days of the week: Wednesday (Odin's day), Thursday (Thor's day), and Friday (Frejya's day). The gods each had their own hall in Asgard, the Land Beyond, and here too was Yggdrasil, the sacred tree of life whose roots held the world together. The idea of a tree being the key to life is one that people could pay attention to today, when acid rain threatens to destroy Europe's forests.

When a Viking chief, or earl, died he was buried in a boat to take him to the next world. Sometimes it would be an actual wooden boat, perhaps the very one in which the earl had gone to battle. Excavations of these buried remains have led to much of our knowledge about Viking ships. On other occasions, the shape of a ship would be marked out on the ground with stones. Many of these stone "ships" remain today and are clearly visible in aerial photography. The grave would be filled with necessities for the next life, particularly helmet, armor, and sword.

Viking religion was a private affair, with individuals worshiping in their own way, and making offerings as they saw fit. There were priests, who might simply be important persons in the townships. In Iceland, the offices of priest and chieftain were combined.

Early Christianity

Just before the year 1000, Christianity began to spread through the Viking kingdoms, helped partly by fears that on this date, known as the millennium, the world would come to an end. In many places Christianity and the earlier religion existed side by side for centuries afterward. A person might worship Christ and yet still make an offering to Thor before going on a sea voyage.

This dual approach to religion is reflected in the decoration of Norway's early churches, a number of which have been preserved. They are made of large timbers, or staves, which give them their name, stave churches. Although not very large, these churches are built reaching up to heaven like the much larger stone churches elsewhere in Europe. A close look, however, shows the Viking tradition continuing, with dragon decorations jutting out from the eaves, and runic inscriptions around the door frames and on the inside panels.

Timber churches are common in Scandinavia, but unfortunately there are few that are very old, because of fire. Those that have survived from early times, particularly in Sweden, are often decorated inside with medieval paintings of saints and biblical scenes. Scandinavia's small population and relative poverty in the Middle Ages mean that there are few of the highly elaborate stone cathedrals that are the treasures of other European countries. The most

This fishermen's church at Vågen, on the Lofoten Islands, is built in the manner of a stave church, with dragon decorations jutting out from the eaves.

impressive ancient stone cathedrals are at Trondheim in Norway and Uppsala in Sweden.

There are plenty of unusual churches, though, some of which are very old. In central Sweden there is Vadstena Abbey, founded by Saint Bridget. Her bones still lie in a wooden coffin in the nearby cloisters, which now form part of a

Helsinki Cathedral is a massive neoclassical building that dominates the skyline of the city.

hotel. In Helsinki, a circular modern church, Temppeliaukio, has been cut into the rock, and the bare boulder faces form the walls.

The spread of Lutheranism

For 500 years, Christians in Scandinavia accepted the spiritual leadership of the pope. In 1517, Martin Luther, a German, called for the reforms that eventually led to the foundation of the Protestant church. Luther's main point was that people are directly responsible to God for their actions, rather than needing a priest to speak on their behalf. This view seemed well suited to the independent Scandinavians. Lutheranism spread rapidly, and today over 90 percent of the population of each Nordic country consider themselves members of the Lutheran Church. Not all of them, of course, are active worshipers.

The Lutheran faith does not favor images of saints, so Scandinavian churches often seem rather bare and severe. This is not true in Finland's northeast, where the Russian influence means that many people worship in Orthodox churches. Like those in Greece and the Soviet Union, these churches are elaborately decorated with icons and ornamentation. There are minority churches in Scandinavia, of course, particularly Jewish synagogues, but the range is limited by the small numbers of immigrants. An exception is Sweden, where the Catholic church is growing because of immigration.

Celebrations in December

Long before they became converted to Christianity, northern people celebrated the shortest day of the year in late December. They wanted to be sure that from then on the days would grow longer until eventually summer returned. The shortest day is still celebrated in Sweden, where Lucia, the queen of light, visits homes. A girl dressed in white with candles on her head, and accompanied by a group of followers, wakes people very early with traditional songs.

Lappland is the traditional home of Santa Claus, and the town of Rovaniemi has become the center of a thriving midwinter tourist attraction. Visitors can see Santa Claus's workshop, ride in sleighs pulled by reindeer, and open their presents in the Arctic twilight.

11 Social Experiments

People from other countries often say that Scandinavian governments have too much influence on people's everyday life. It is true, for example, that except for weak beer, Scandinavians can only buy alcoholic drinks to take home from special stores run by the state. Laws against drunken driving are very strict. Also, taxes on people's earnings are very high.

On the other hand, the help given to people by the state in health, welfare, and education is often much greater than in the United States, in other European countries, or in Australia.

This concern for welfare extends to people in prison. Scandinavians believe that prisons should attempt to reform criminals, not just lock them away. Sweden pioneered open prisons, where prisoners are encouraged to study and are often allowed out for short holidays.

Health and welfare

Throughout Scandinavia, there are many very modern, well-equipped hospitals. Treatment is usually "free" to the individual because costs are paid out of everyone's taxes. However, patients going to a doctor's office pay a part of both the fee and the cost of drugs.

Health services are linked closely with welfare provision. For working parents there are some of the best child-care facilities in the world. For people out of work, benefit payments are good, but often an unemployed person may have to undertake a retraining program. State pensions

These Danish children are enjoying a visit to the Tivoli Gardens in Copenhagen. They have been brought up in a society with some of the best health care and welfare facilities in the world. They can look forward to being well cared for right into their old age.

are generous, particularly in Sweden, but it is common to work until the age of 67 or older.

It is often argued that people will not want to work if the state provides high unemployment benefits and good health and welfare programs. Scandinavia proves these arguments wrong. In spite of the high taxation needed to pay for all the benefits, people still work hard and have a high standard of living. Also, Scandinavia is almost completely free of poverty, and of people begging or sleeping on the streets.

Housing

Since World War II, there has been a big shift of population into the cities. In Denmark, for example, 21 percent of the working population was employed in agriculture in 1950, but only 4.3 percent was by 1986. Most new jobs have been in the factories on the edge of towns and cities, many of which have doubled their population since 1945. This movement of people has put a constant pressure on city housing.

There are strict planning laws to prevent suburban sprawl and almost all new housing projects take the form of tall buildings. Often the apartment buildings have drive-in garages underneath. The demand for housing means that people still have to put up with fairly small apartments. Icelanders, curiously, have done well, having moved in 50 years from traditional turf-roofed cottages to apartments larger than the Scandinavian average.

Of course, not all new housing is made up of high-rise buildings. Denmark, in particular, has experimented with mixed housing where family houses are built side by side with small groups of apartments and complexes specially designed for elderly people. In the newest developments, elderly people are housed in the ground-floor apartments of a mixed building.

State and local government are often involved in housing projects, while the idea of housing cooperatives has spread from Denmark. It is possible to borrow money fairly cheaply through "housing banks," and Scandinavians usually own their own home rather than rent it.

Education

The early Lutheran church insisted on the importance of education. Finns were virtually forced to become literate when a law of 1686

In Scandinavia all children enjoy classes in many subjects, like these Finnish boys learning to cook.

required them to read before they were allowed to marry. Compulsory state education began as early as 1814 in Denmark and 1827 in Norway. Partly as a result, private schools charging tuition make up only about three percent of the total schools in Denmark, Norway, and Sweden.

Finland has had more private schools because, historically, state schools had to teach all lessons in Swedish. Finns who wanted their children taught in their own language had to set up their own schools. Today, only about a third of the schools are state schools. However, almost all the rest are owned by local communities so that children still get a free education.

Language teaching is very important, because Scandinavians know that when they go abroad, probably no one will speak their language. English is the most common second language, and is taught beginning at the age of nine. However, children will frequently learn a third language chosen from French, German, Spanish, or Russian. It is rare to find an adult Scandinavian who does not speak at least a little English, and many can speak three languages.

At the secondary level, schools begin to concentrate on training related to jobs. They emphasize skills like agriculture or forestry. Special Saami schools, such as those at Karasjokk and Jokkmokk, emphasize traditional Saami arts and crafts. One type of school is unique to Scandinavia, and this is the Folk High School. It is a kind of adult residential school for students over 18. Some Folk High Schools have specialized courses related to people's jobs, such as nursing and fishing.

Scandinavia has had universities for many centuries. Uppsala University was founded in 1477 and Copenhagen University in 1479. Today, many school graduates go on to a university.

The importance given to education is illustrated by the Students' Day celebrations. This happens on different days in the different countries, when the streets are thronged with students wearing special white caps that show that they have passed their university entrance examination. Noisy and enthusiastic celebrations go on for several nights.

12 The Scandinavian Life-style

Scandinavians like to get away from the cities whenever possible. The picturesque Göta Canal in Sweden is a great attraction, either to ride on or just watch the boats going through the locks.

The practicality of the Scandinavian people shows itself in the way they learn to live with the harsh conditions of winter and make the most of summer. Perhaps it is living in a cramped city apartment, enduring long hours of darkness for so much of the year, that makes Scandinavians eager to enjoy summer outdoors. They seem to have a stronger need than most people to get away from the city and live close to nature.

Allemannsrett

This need to be close to nature is summed up in a law unique to Norway and Sweden called Allemannsrett. Literally, it means "everybody's right," and can best be translated as "right of access." Basically, it means anyone can go anywhere in the countryside. Crops must be respected and other people's homes must not be approached too closely, but apart from that, there are no laws against trespassing, and no signs saying "trespassers will be prosecuted." So an escape from city life is made easy by the Allemannsrett, and it also allows walkers to pick berries and mushrooms as they wish. The Scandinavians think that the natural fruits of the countryside are for all to enjoy.

Summer "huts"

Many Scandinavians deliberately live in a tiny city apartment in order to be able to afford a comparatively luxurious summer house "up in the mountains" (for Norwegians), or "on one of the islands" (for Swedes). Second homes are not necessarily a sign of great wealth. A third of all Finnish families have a summer house.

The word for these wooden houses is like the English word "hut." In fact, they are not at all hut-like. Often they are as big as a city apartment in the United States or a main family home in Europe or Australia and are well equipped with a shower and even a sauna.

The sauna

After exercise, or just for relaxation, Scandinavians have a special treat: the sauna bath. This cure for colds, invented by the Finns, spread across Scandinavia and beyond.

A sauna is a wooden room, traditionally heated by a charcoal stove, but today by an electric stove, until the temperature is very high. Often the stove is also the only lighting. Whole families go into their sauna, to bake naked in the heat. In public saunas, men and women have separate rooms. Public or private, the sauna is not just for sweating; it is a relaxing social occasion. In the half-darkness, people unwind and enjoy a chat.

Some people take birch twigs, collected the summer before and with the dried leaves still on them, into the sauna. When the twigs are gently slapped against the skin, it helps open the pores so the body sweats freely. Sometimes a little water is thrown on the stove so that the sauna becomes very humid. Herbs or eucalyptus may be added to give a pleasant smell.

Finally, it is time to cool down. In a public sauna, this could mean a dive into a swimming pool. In remote places, people may roll in the snow or even take a short dip in an icy lake. It sounds strange and painful, but the sudden chilling seems to seal the heat into the body and people glow with good health.

Sports

Although Scandinavians are good at skiing and generally concerned with fitness, the climate and landscape are not suited to other sports. There are very few soccer fields, for example. Gymnasiums and indoor tennis courts are much more common. Also, perhaps because of the small populations, there have been relatively few

Sports Facts

- Paavo Nurmi was a Finnish middle- and long-distance runner who held 24 world records in the 1920s, including the mile and the marathon.

- Norway has been the most successful country in men's Olympic speed skating, with 18 wins up to 1984.

- Ingemar Stenmark of Sweden has won three Alpine Slalom championships.

- Björn Borg of Sweden won the Junior Wimbledon tennis title in 1972, and the Wimbledon Men's Tennis Singles for five years between 1976 and 1980. He won the French championships six times between 1974 and 1981. Since Borg's victories, several other Swedes have become famous in tennis, notably Mats Wilander and Stefan Edberg.

- Orienteering, cross-country foot races in which racers have to use a compass and map, was invented by Major Ernst Killander of Sweden in 1918. The sport is still dominated by Scandinavians.

internationally recognized sportsmen and women, at least until recently.

Skiing

Many summer houses have double-glazed windows, insulation, and heating so they can also be used for winter skiing weekends. The first sleet flurries come in October, and by January three to seven feet of snow has fallen. In the cold temperatures, the snow becomes hard and

Scandinavian Ski Firsts
- The first known ski was found in Höting, Sweden, and is about 6,500 years old.
- The first competition for skiing as a sport was held at Tromsø, Norway, in 1843.
- The first competitive ski jumping was from the top of a cow-shed at Drontheim, Norway, in 1797.

Skiing is very popular both as a sport and a way of travel. Cross-country skiing is the most popular, although for the more intrepid there is also downhill racing.

compact, and good for skiing. Over newly fallen snow, skiing can be hard work, so around ski resorts a kind of tractor pulls a special plow to make a ski-track or *piste*. Skiing in these grooves is easier and faster.

In the past, almost all Scandinavians, except

the Danish, learned to ski when very young. For many children it was the only way to go to school. Today, city life and snowplows mean that large numbers of children grow up without learning to ski. Some Scandinavians worry that this will mean the loss of an important part of Nordic life.

The small size of most towns and cities means that skiing is close at hand for people who enjoy it. The northern suburbs of Oslo, for example, are close to Nordmarka, the North Forest. City workers start and finish work early so they can get home in the mid-afternoon, and within minutes be on a forest trail with hardly anyone in sight. In midwinter they may meet an elk or the king of Norway who often skis in Nordmarka, having bought his ticket for the Holmenkøllen train.

Winter life

The Norwegian city of Hammerfest seems to sum up the Scandinavian way of life. As the most northerly city in the world, it is well inside the Arctic Circle. It has been a fishing port for several hundred years and people have learned to live both with the joy of sunshine all night long in summer and the two months of constant winter darkness. When electric lighting was invented, Hammerfest was the first town to light its streets in 1891. The same Scandinavian practicality was shown when the German army knocked most of the town to the ground, and the people of Hammerfest got busy and rebuilt it. This adaptability seems typical, and perhaps the essence of being Scandinavian is the ability to cope with winter with all the resourcefulness and independence that it requires.

Index

© Heinemann Children's Reference 1990
This edition orginally published 1990 by
Heinemann Children's Reference, a division
of Heinemann Educational Books, Ltd.